📖 SCHOLASTIC

Science SuperGiants

What Makes the Light Bright, Thomas Edison?

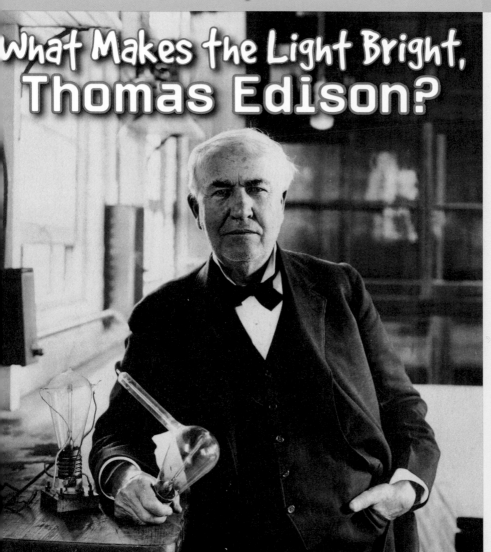

Melvin and Gilda Berger

illustrated by Brand

SCHOLASTIC 💡 NON

an imprint of

📖 SCHOLASTIC

D1005328

Contents

How did Thomas Edison change the world?

Thomas Alva Edison invented the electric lightbulb in 1879. The bulb took the place of the gas lamp. Gas lamps had many problems. They were smoky, smelled bad, and sometimes started fires.

Edison also found a way to bring electricity to everyone. He built huge machines, called dynamos, to produce the electricity. Long wires carried the electricity from the dynamos to people's homes and businesses.

Thanks to Edison, we now have lights to change night into day, and electricity to run our TVs, computers, refrigerators, and air conditioners. The world would be a very different place without Thomas Alva Edison.

Thomas Alva Edison in 1912 holding the electric lightbulb.

Did Edison invent electricity?

No. No one invented electricity. Electricity is a form of energy that is found in nature. The Greeks knew about electricity almost 2,500 years ago. In the eighteenth century, Benjamin Franklin flew a kite during a lightning storm to prove that lightning is a form of electricity.

Many people had tried to use electricity before Edison. Some even made electric lights, but none worked very well.

Edison wanted to be the first person to invent an electric light that worked well and cost little. He also wanted to be the first person to build a power plant to bring electricity to a city.

In June, 1752, Benjamin Franklin showed that lightning is electricity by flying a kite in a storm. Lightning struck the kite wire and traveled down to the key (near the end), where it caused a spark. In 1876, Currier & Ives created this image of Franklin's experiment.

When and where was Edison born?

Thomas Alva Edison was born on February 11, 1847, in Milan, Ohio. His parents were Samuel and Nancy Elliot Edison. They had seven children. Thomas was the youngest. Everyone called him Al, which was short for Alva.

This red brick house in Milan, Ohio, was Thomas Alva Edison's birthplace and boyhood home.

Al was a very curious child. He had a knack for getting into trouble. At the age of six, Al set fire to his father's barn. He said it was "just to see what it would do." Of course, his father was very angry.

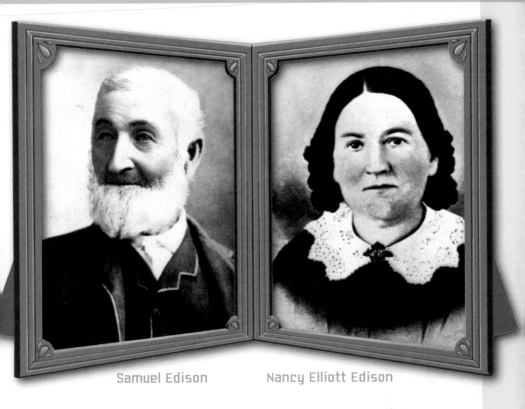

Samuel Edison   Nancy Elliott Edison

In 1854, the family moved to Port Huron, Michigan. Mr. Edison tried different businesses. None worked out very well. The family did not have much money.

Edison at age three.

Was Edison a good student?

Edison was not a very good student. He did not start school until he was seven years old. That's because he was sick a lot. His classmates thought he wasn't smart because he refused to speak up in class. After only three months he dropped out. His mother, who had been a school teacher, began teaching him at home.

When Al was nine, his mother bought him a science book. He fell in love with chemistry and set up a science laboratory in the basement of his house. Day after day, Al tried the experiments in the book. He bought lots of chemicals and put them into glass bottles that he marked POISON. It was Al's way of making sure that no one touched his things!

Did Edison have trouble hearing?

Edison was deaf in his left ear and could barely hear with his right one. Poor hearing ran in his family. Frequent childhood illnesses probably made his hearing even worse.

Edison later wrote, "I have not heard a bird sing since I was twelve years old."

Around the age of twelve, Al got a job selling newspapers and candy on the trains of the Grand Trunk Railway. In his free moments he did experiments in the train's

Al at work on the railroad. Notice how different trains looked.

baggage car. One day, a jar of chemicals fell and started a small fire. The furious conductor struck the boy on his ears. That, too, may have damaged Al's hearing.

When did Edison save someone's life?

After the fire in the baggage car, Edison lost his job. However, he continued to sell newspapers at stations along the railway route.

According to one story, young Edison saw a three-year-old boy walking on a track. A train was coming toward him. Edison ran over and whisked the boy away. The boy's father was the telegraph operator at the station. He wanted to thank Edison for saving his son's life, so he offered to teach Edison how to work a telegraph. Edison couldn't wait to start.

Young Edison at age fourteen.

This wood engraving illustrates the story of Edison saving a young boy at the Mt. Clemens, Michigan, railroad station.

What was Edison's first invention?

Edison's first invention improved the telegraph. By age sixteen, he was working as a railroad telegrapher. At that time, there were no telephones or computers. People kept in touch by telegraph. Operators tapped out messages that traveled long distances through electrical wires. The electricity came from batteries. The messages were in a code of dots and dashes, called the Morse code.

Edison's duty was to tap out a message every half hour to show that he was awake. Edison found it very hard to stay up all night. So he hooked up a clock to the telegraph. Now, messages went out automatically every half hour — no operator necessary! This was Edison's first invention.

In his years as a railroad telegrapher, Edison not only had to tap out messages into Morse code and translate those that he received, but also had to keep the equipment running. Therefore, Edison was able to learn a lot about electricity, how batteries worked, and how to wire circuits.

What did Edison invent next?

By 1868, Edison was living in Boston. There he invented an electric vote-counting machine. It was the first of 1,093 patents that Edison would get.

A patent is a document issued by a government. It says that only the inventor can make, use, or sell the invention. Unfortunately, few people seemed to need or want the vote counter.

In 1869, Edison arrived in New York City with only one dollar in his pocket. A friend let Edison sleep in his office. When the office's telegraph machine broke, Edison fixed it. Later, he invented a better telegraph machine. To protect the invention, Edison got a patent. The owner of the office bought the patent for $40,000. Edison was now a rich man.

T. A. EDISON,
Electric Vote-Recorder.

No. 90,646,

Patented June 1, 1869.

Witnesses.
Carroll D. Wright
DeWitt C. Roberts

Inventor.
Thomas A. Edison.

Right: The drawing from Edison's first patent application for an electric vote-recording machine.
Left: Edison intended his vote recorder to be used by Congress, but they felt it would be too slow.

When did Edison become a full-time inventor?

In the winter of 1870, Edison became a full-time inventor. He used the money from the telegraph patent sale to start his own company in Newark, New Jersey, making "inventions to order." Edison hired a team of men to help him invent things that people asked for.

The Newark workshop turned out several important inventions. Edison found ways to send as many as four telegraph messages through the same wire at the same time! He invented wax paper. He also built a better typewriter with metal parts instead of wood.

Edison often worked day and night — and expected his workers to do the same.

This photo of Edison's first factory, taken in 1873, shows the large team of expert workers that Edison hired and posed outside the workshop.

Edison's Newark Factory Ward St. 1873.

Was Edison married?

Yes. Twice. In 1871, at age twenty-four, Edison met sixteen-year-old Mary Stilwell. During their courtship, Edison taught Mary the Morse code. This way, they could "talk," and no one would know what they were saying. The couple married on Christmas Day of that year.

In 1876, Edison bought a house and land in Menlo Park, New Jersey. It was not far from

Mary Stilwell

A .−	K −.−	U ..−	5 .....
B −...	L .−..	V ...−	6 −....
C −.−.	M −−	W .−−	7 −−...
D −..	N −.	X −..−	8 −−−..
E .	O −−−	Y −.−−	9 −−−−.
F ..−.	P .−−.	Z −−..	0 −−−−−
G −−.	Q −−.−	1 .−−−−	? ..−−..
H	R .−.	2 ..−−−	. .−.−.−
I ..	S ...	3 ...−−	, −−..−−
J .−−−	T −	4 ....−	

The dots and dashes of Morse code.

Newark. The house had lots of room for Mary and their growing children, Marion, Thomas Jr., and William.

Edison loved his wife and children. However, he spent so much time in his workshop that he was rarely home. His absence left Mary feeling sad and lonely.

This is the second-floor laboratory of
Edison's Menlo Park "invention factory."

What was Edison's "invention factory"?

It was the big, new workshop Edison built next to his house in Menlo Park. His goal was to bring out a "minor invention every ten days and a big thing every six months or so." The goal seemed impossible, but Edison did just that. In fact, he invented so many things that people called him the "Wizard of Menlo Park."

More than twenty people worked for Edison. They were a very talented group. Each one had a special skill to help Edison build his inventions.

What important inventions did Edison make at Menlo Park?

One of Edison's many important inventions was an improved telephone. Alexander Graham Bell had invented the telephone in 1876. Using Bell's phone, you had to shout to be heard. Edison fine-tuned the phone so that normal voices could be heard loud and clear. It was also Edison's idea to say "hello" when answering the telephone.

Edison's favorite invention, however, was the phonograph — a machine to record and play back sounds. In 1877, Edison made the first one. It was a soda-can-sized cylinder wrapped in a thin sheet of tinfoil. On each side was a short tube with a pin at the end. Edison turned the cylinder and shouted, "Mary had a little lamb," into one tube. The sound vibrations shook the pin and made a long groove in the tinfoil.

To play back the sound, Edison turned the cylinder again. Out came "Mary had a little lamb." The phonograph worked!

The photo shows a working model of Edison's first phonograph. Note the handle to turn the cylinder and the lines scratched in the tinfoil by the pin.

When did Edison start work on the electric lightbulb?

In 1879, Edison decided to invent a long-burning electric lightbulb. For thirty years, people had tried to do the same thing. They had all failed. The usual way was to pass electricity through a wire inside a glass bulb. This wire is called a filament. When electricity passes through, the filament gets so hot that it glows with a bright light.

Earlier inventors tried many kinds of filaments. Every one had the same problem. The light lasted a few moments at most. Some filaments just burned up. A few melted.

Edison set out to find the right filament that would give light *and* last a long time.

Edison heated every possible filament material to see which ones could take the most heat.

How did Edison find the best filament?

Edison knew that long, thin filaments burn brighter than thicker filaments. So he made his filaments as thin as possible. He formed the filaments into long, tight coils so they would give the most light. He also knew that most filaments would burn up in the air. So he pumped all the air out of the bulbs.

Edison tried hundreds of different filaments. He experimented with

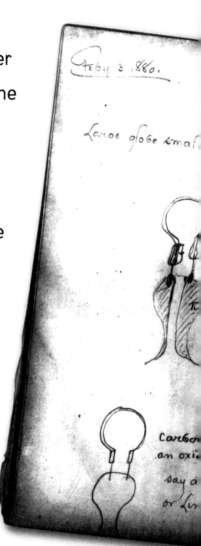

filaments made of metal, wood, cardboard, plants, thread — and even hair from a man's beard. Finally, after two years of failure, Edison found what he was looking for — a long-lasting filament.

Notice the long, thin filament in the shape of a small horseshoe.

What was the best filament?

The most successful filament was made of cotton thread. But not just any thread. It was thread that Edison first slowly heated in an oven. The heat changed the cotton into a chemical called carbon.

All summer, Edison worked to improve the carbon filament. Finally, on the night of October 19, 1879, he had it. Edison turned on a lamp with the new carbon filament. The light grew brighter and brighter. It gave as much light as thirty candles. Edison wrote, ". . . the sight we had so long desired to see met our eyes." It was the first long-lasting electric light! It burned for more than thirteen hours.

A replica of Edison's first successful lightbulb.

Are fluorescent lightbulbs like other bulbs?

No. Fluorescent bulbs do not have filaments. They are long, thin, glass tubes coated with chemicals and filled with gases. Electricity flows through the gases. This makes the chemicals coating the tube give off light.

Several engineers developed the fluorescent lightbulb about sixty years after Edison invented the electric lightbulb. Fluorescents use less electricity and produce less heat than electric lightbulbs. Most schools, stores, and offices now use fluorescent light.

Flourescent lights make this underground subway station look like the daytime 24/7.

When did Edison learn to produce electricity?

During the 1880s, Edison and his workers at Menlo Park built two huge generators. Generators are giant machines that are run mostly by steam. They produce electricity. In Edison's time, the generators were called dynamos. Workers laid 15 miles (24 km) of wire. The wire went from the generators to all the buildings in a ten-block area in New York City.

On September 4, 1882, Edison was ready to test the system. He gave the signal.

A worker pulled the switch. Instantly hundreds of electric lights burst into brightness. It was the beginning of the electric age.

The first dynamo on Pearl Street, New York City. It supplied power to light 800 of Edison's newly invented electric lightbulbs.

Try it out!

Experiment #1: See how a modern lightbulb works.

You'll need a flashlight with a bulb.

1. Look closely at the flashlight's bulb.

2. Find the tiny filament in the middle of the bulb.

2. Turn on the flashlight while looking at the filament.

3. Turn off the flashlight, still looking at the filament.

The filament is a thin, coiled wire made of the metal tungsten. That's the part of the bulb in the flashlight that makes the light. What happens to the filament when you turn on the flashlight? It does not move. It does not change shape. Yet it very quickly gets hot, begins to glow, and gives off light. When you turn off the flashlight, the light disappears. The filament is dark again.

Try it out!

Experiment #2: Trace the flow of electricity inside a flashlight.

You'll need a flashlight with a battery.

1. Unscrew a flashlight.

2. Find the battery (or batteries inside).

3. Find the two wires or metal parts that go from the battery to the bulb.

The flashlight's battery is its source of electricity. It is like the generator in a power plant. One wire or metal part carries the electricity to the bulb. The other takes the electricity back to the battery. The wires, battery, and bulb make a big loop. They meet at the on-off switch.

The electric lights in your house work like the flashlight. Electricity comes into your house through wires. It flows into the bulbs and then back to the generator.

In 1884, Edison's wife, Mary, died. It was a terrible blow to the inventor. He stopped going to work in his Menlo Park lab. But he continued to build power plants in cities. Two

years later, Edison married Mina Miller, the young daughter of Lewis Miller, a fellow inventor and manufacturer. Thomas and Mina had three

Mina Miller with daughter, Madeleine

The West Orange, New Jersey, home of Thomas Edison, now a national historic site.

children — Charles, Madeleine, and Theodore.

In 1887, Edison set up a larger lab in West Orange, New Jersey. Here, Edison started working again: He found a way to separate iron ore from rocks. He perfected a movie camera and a projector. He also came up with a safety lamp that a miner could wear on his helmet.

Did Edison invent motion pictures?

Edison was one of several inventors in the 1880s who tried to make and show motion pictures. Edison said that he wanted to "do for the Eye what the phonograph does for the Ear." He finally succeeded in 1889. No one is sure if he was first.

Edison developed two machines: a camera (kinetograph) for taking a number of separate pictures on a long strip of film, and a machine (kinetoscope) to show the pictures. The roll of film passed through the kinetoscope at high speed. A person watching through a peephole saw the pictures move.

Edison's West Orange studio, called Black Maria, was the first motion picture studio in America.

Using a kinetoscpe, the man is viewing moving pictures. Kinetoscope parlors, offering a choice of films, first opened in New York and London in 1894.

When did Edison die?

Edison died on October 18, 1931. He was eighty-four years old. Herbert Hoover was President. On the day of Edison's funeral, President Hoover asked people all over America to dim the lights in their homes. It was a very fitting tribute to Edison.

Most people agree that Edison's greatest invention was the electric lightbulb. In fact, he obtained patents for more than one thousand different inventions. They range from the early vote-counting machine to secret work he did for the U.S. Navy in the final years of his life.

Edison said, "The trouble with other inventors is that they try a few things and they quit. I never quit until I get what I want." That's a very good lesson for us all!

Edison claimed his deafness gave him more time to work and helped him focus better than he could otherwise. In spite of his poor hearing, he enjoyed music and said he could hear music "through the skull."

Edison time line

1847	Thomas Alva Edison born in Milan, Ohio, on February 11
1854	Family moves to Port Huron, Michigan; Edison starts school, but drops out after three months
1856	Mother buys Edison a chemistry book; he tries all the experiments
1859	Gets job selling newspapers and snacks on Grand Trunk Railway; he sets train car on fire doing experiment
1863	Starts work as a telegraph operator; invents device to send telegraph messages without operator
1868	Moves to Boston, invents an automatic vote-counter and gets first patent
1869	Moves to New York City; becomes a full-time inventor
1870	Opens workshop in Newark, New Jersey; improves the typewriter
1871	Marries Mary Stilwell

1876	Alexander Graham Bell invents the telephone
1876	Edison opens his lab in Menlo Park, New Jersey
1877	Improves the telephone and invents the phonograph
1879	Invents electric lightbulb
1882	Opens power plant to supply electricity to part of New York City
1884	Wife Mary dies
1886	Marries Mina Miller
1887	Builds bigger, more modern lab in West Orange, New Jersey
1889	Invents the movie camera
1897	Invites public to see projector that shows movies
1913-1915	Connects phonograph and movie camera to make talking movies; does not succeed and drops project
1927-1931	Works on secret inventions for the U.S. Navy
1929	National celebration of the fiftieth anniversary of the electric light
1931	Dies in West Orange, New Jersey, on October 18

Index

Photo Credits: US Department of the Interior/National Park Service/Edison National Historic Site: 4, 9 [top], 18, 21, 22, 37, 40, 45; Museum of the City of New York/CORBIS: 7; The Granger Collection, NY, NY: 8; 9 [bottom], 13, 27, 33; CORBIS: 14, 15; Ford Archives/Henry Ford Museum: 24; Gettyimages, NY, NY: 34; Joseph Sohm; ChromoSohm Inc./CORBIS: 41; Science and Society Picture Library/London: 42.

Text copyright © 2006 by Melvin and Gilda Berger
Illustrations copyright © 2006 by Brandon Dorman
All rights reserved. Published by Scholastic Inc., *Publishers since 1920.*

Library of Congress cataloguing-in-publication data available.

ISBN 10: 0-439-83380-9 ISBN 13: 978-0-439-83380-6

10 9 8 7 6 5 4 3 2 1   07 08 09 10

Printed in the U.S.A. • First printing, November 2006
Book design by Nancy Sabato